AT LAGUNITAS

With Other Poems

AT LAGUNITAS

With Other Poems

PETER DECHERT

SANTA FE

© 2008 by Peter Dechert. All rights reserved.

No part of this book may be reproduced in any form or by any electronic or mechanical means including information storage and retrieval systems without permission in writing from the publisher, except by a reviewer who may quote brief passages in a review.

Sunstone books may be purchased for educational, business, or sales promotional use. For information please write:
Special Markets Department, Sunstone Press,
P.O. Box 2321, Santa Fe, New Mexico 87504-2321.

Library of Congress Cataloging-in-Publication Data

Dechert, Peter, 1924-
  At Lagunitas ; with other poems / Peter Dechert.
    p. cm.
  ISBN 978-0-86534-617-8 (alk. paper) -- ISBN 978-0-86534-618-5 (pbk. : alk. paper)
  I. Title.

PS3604.E239A95 2008
811'.6--dc22
                                                    2007043203

WWW.SUNSTONEPRESS.COM
SUNSTONE PRESS / POST OFFICE BOX 2321 / SANTA FE, NM 87504-2321 /USA
(505) 988-4418 / ORDERS ONLY (800) 243-5644 / FAX (505) 988-1025

This Collection Is For

My Family

and also for

Friends Made and Lost During a Lifetime

and for

A Pal

TABLE OF CONTENTS

(Assembled in alphabetical order)

Again and Always and the Stars	9
And in the Name of Science	11
And Vanishes	12
An Equivalence	13
As If	14
At Lagunitas	15
Bereft	17
Blind Mice	18
Blocks	19
Breeze	20
Child of Ice	21
Circus	22
Crocus	23
Dagonet	24
Daisy	25
Decline of a Falstaff	29
Donald's Well	34
Dusk Storm	35
Emeralds	36
Emotion Does Not Derive from Any Form	37
Enthralled	38
Evocation	39
Fugue: October	40
Go Out in Anger	41
Heroism	42
Hitrun	43
Holiday from Camelot	44
In Another Country	45
In State	47
I Shall Think of You on Christmas Morning	48
It Is Not for Nothing	49
Jill's Answer	50
Jungle Gym	51
Kobaleski	52
Krinkelt: 1945	53

Life's Little Lessons	54
Maybelle	55
The Mountains Over Mora	56
The Mulberry Bush	58
Old Man	59
On Days When I Watch Ashes in Your Eyes	62
One Kind of Requiem	63
On Hope's Eightieth Birthday	64
Only by Words	66
Partir *and* On the Other Hand	67
Paul Rejected	70
Playmates	71
Poem 81	72
Poem for John Meem	73
Poets Are Paltry People	74
Recalling Astolat	76
Reunion	77
Rose Song	78
Sailboats Into Eclipse	79
The Seafarer	80
Shadows for Shadows	82
Showering	83
Snow in Middle Autumn	85
Some Things that Break	86
"Song, Made in Lieu of Many Ornaments"	87
Suddenly	88
Teddy's Crow	89
Tell Me No Lies of Roses in the Streets	91
Time Robs	92
To Create the Gull	93
To the Wind in Fragments	94
Two Sorts of Trees	96
Waiting for Rain	97
War Marriage at Shelby	99
What I Remember from My War	100
When the Winds Come	101
The Wife's Lament	102
Wishing Well	104
Yesterdays : Tomorrows	105
Afterword	107

Again and Always and the Stars

again and always and the stars
turn over earth and wear away
what things we know or thought we knew
our years our decades all the words

that we may speak or might have spoken
till we are phantoms lost in time
frail phantoms that cannot survive
alternative eternities

and what we do and speak today
will be no history at all
when forests fade to buried coal
and sunlit coastlines freeze to bays

with new liquidities of ice
where once we bathed our dreams of love
desire and sorrow joy dismay
warm promises beyond our keeping

for histories must come and go
and in each transience of time
forever is not integral
to what was once and what will be

when history renews itself
with unanticipated phantoms
whose novel logic may express
new modes of always and again

but still this now we know today
holds all the lifetimes we can know
in this eternity of ours
in which we dream our own forevers

these years these decades all our words
not yet inconsequential
                                though
again and always and the stars
turn over earth and wear away

And in the Name of Science

                          no thought of stars
I looking south from this portal beyond
Santa Fe, over deep Cerrillos
to Sandias, dark Ortiz, blue San Pedros, all
mountains, pastel sky, idle illusions
of an amateur wizard.
           Age seeps some evenings
through my foundations, I am being drowned
by wells supposed to dry up, I would give
whatever I have to give not to have to give it.

I have been known to lecture
communication at idiots, photography at blind men,
living to corpses.
        And in the name of science
I suppose I could ask
fragrant old ladies to finger delicate bones
of skeletons long in earth, to admire the mica
arrows in the crania of their ancestors.
      In the name of something
I could show them artifacts from their very graves,
but they never ask. Or is it
they never ask without thinking
they are beautiful? Is it better that I
associate from guts, from liver, from sphincter?
From what heart? So many poets said it
it must be wrong.
        No thought of stars, no
no thought really but watching
whatever may happen beyond those clouds, next, half
listening to my daughter, to Caroline saying things
her sisters said, that my sisters
used to say: things so new
so suddenly old I will not think about them

And Vanishes

Suspended and diluted by the sky
for a still moment the bird
soars free, dips
                    and vanishes
beyond the rim of the canyon. I stand
in the sun, nothing has passed, the world
spirals through voids as it must always do:
I with it. Only the memory
hangs in my mind, floating, of a bird.

An Equivalence

It is
as if
you looked
through a sudden
window
and the poem
stared back at you.

You see
it. You
could make
its photograph.

Only the words are hard.

Speak
to it: you
get no more answer
than twilight
gives
to the blackbird
calling.

Speak
of it: none
but the foolishly
brave
speak of it:
idiots,
poets
risking
themselves against all of forever
on the loss of it.

As If

Old fondnesses decayed to air
that we breathe and that others breathe,
what they were is lost to us
beyond all power to retrieve:

encountering each other now
we view ourselves as strangers lost,
momentary enemies
when one must take the footpath first;

and cautiously we talk of things,
wishing the other far away,
while wisps of memory that block
our yesterdays from this today

erode what old humanity
remained to bind us not in two,
as if one accident of eyes
is all that chance intends to do.

At Lagunitas

Whisper what it is
this evening: late light
among gold leaves, and the lakes
dusk in an array of prisms.
The lakes are sometimes suddenly circular
with fish rising;
migrating birds come slowly
with a larger hush among the stillness
to be heard. The trees lean silver: whisper
what it is.

                Cañada del Oso,
Lobo Canyon, Beehive Spring, animals
and insects all forgotten now: bear, wolf
swarm beyond the saddles of mountains
and I wonder (once upon a time noticing
how some girls, even the prettiest perhaps,
will walk by slowly
and then slowly look back behind them
to judge the impression they have made);

for the leaves here in their colors
turn past on the slow air, growing
older at each nightfall, waiting:
waiting for one night when the long wind
will wake like a sleepy prince, and notice.
Oh, they reach, lost rays, old eyes that glint
in the sunset back among the leaves, they reach
through the twilight as if they were saying
we are not gone yet, we have put ourselves all
together in colors of autumn coming.

And the sun goes, a cold night tendril
drifts below my ear, sting
of an aging bee, wisp of circular wind
for leaves at last to dance on
in the evening, fluttering north
like coquettish old maids from a ball.
Well, it is the end of still another season:
whisper me what it is.

Bereft

sits in dark corners, bars,
renounces violence,
lets beard grow long, makes friends
and loses them. Lover
gone. When roaming streets
is offered love of many sorts, broken
hearted love
engaged in, flesh willing, spirit gone.
Each day succession nights.
Forgets to sleep
in ten-bit movies. Drink, name it,
all the same
                poor butterfly
when your lover has gone   why won't
someone send a tender
blue boy
                channel full of ice
much too cold, railroads running too
far behind schedule to depend
on rumbling underfoot even in tavern
where friend once came. Hell with friend
to hell with lover:
lies down, bed springy, forty-five much too big

father always said coward

Blind Mice

Jack: be nimble and be quick
when you know the sky is falling,
take your candlestick with you
if you must go calling.

Should you happen on blind mice
what you learn may be surprising:
Jack, keep proud of blinded mice
when the moon is rising,

you must bait your traps for them
only in a sunlit season,
mice die harder in the moon,
and they have their reason:

moonlight suits dark vision well
while they charm the stars to blind you;
there is no enchanted girl
then will come and find you,

no enchantment and no kiss
to awake you from your weeping
on the dream of what mice do
when you might be sleeping,

so be nimble, Jack, be quick
if you hear blind mice at playing:
light your candle in the dark,
curse before your praying.

Blocks

Youngster, I was given
a wooden wagon packed with blocks of wood,
cubes, with which I began by building
small castles, or sometimes walls with ramparts
for my lead soldiers. On each face of each block
were letters, six different letters to every cube,
and I learned to spell my name, PETER,
and the name of our dog ROWDY. Next, sentences:
PETER LOVES ROWDY. My magic cubes were squares
with rounded edges and carefully blunted corners.
I could not hurt my self with them, only learn.

Somewhat elderly these days, things past
have hardened into distinct blocks of time,
discontinuous translucent cubes: each facet
a different interpretation of its event, of what there was
inside. I have outgrown certainty, I guess;
there are no smooth corners here:
eight sharp points to every cube,
twelve cutting edges. Events revisited
no longer playthings, these present blocks
are dangerous to toy with: there is often
much pain from them, much learning left too late.

Breeze

Breeze blows;
Whither it goes
No one knows.

Whence it came?
The same.

Child of Ice

While the north wind
flickers again among the pillars
of your winter palace
blue stars drill
with ruthless accuracy
into the November
of your cold content
and your bare feet like meteors
crack the leaves' last bones.

Circus

Still fresh from victories on the Exchange,
Burton ascends temporary rows
of benches, finds his seat of power, throws
a paper dart, establishing the range.
About him, rustic members of the Grange,
in town today to see heroic shows,
are unconvinced by Burton's regal pose:
he buys a bag of popcorn, which seems strange. . .

Trajan, triumphator, tosses down
a linen mappa; while his senators
plan for Ctesiphon and Persian shores
he meets the obligations of his crown. . . . .
And Burton sails another dart, then roars
to see the sudden entrance of the clown.

Crocus

who stole my blanket and the wispy coat
of brown I bought for winter in the fall
   and what's that little green arm   someone spoke

just like a robin   oh I guess I ought
to take a look around   stop pushing me
you little greensot elbower   the lawn

has spice enough for both of us for weeks
and weeks still   there's a deal of liquor left
   you'll see   another drink and you'll repeat

somebody else's error and bloom in bed
quite red   another one and I'll be tight
too   won't you come into my spider said

the parlor to the fly   say look   it's I
reciting poetry   some more to drink
   now that you ask I will   earthworm goodbye

it's spring spring spring spring spring
it's time we all get drunk on demon spring

Dagonet

Suppose I tell the king he is no king
where most he would be king tonight, and for
all time to come; suppose I make him think

unhappy thoughts or theories no one ought
ever to have to face so unprepared
as he is now; suppose I tell him all

by telling him less than enough to make
him think me entertaining or the fool
sufficiently tonight; suppose I prate

not well enough but wisely in this room
which he has gilded royally for the queen
who is no queen of his, the queen for whom

he is no longer king? Humor is deep
enough to wrench or loose a crown tonight
if twisted so that that which merely seems

to be could really be a fact of life
without exaggeration: there are notes
that would not shimmer on these walls like lights

if I should sing them now, and he would know
my songs had less of music than of truth
in them if he should hear uncertain tones

sung by a fool who always has been fool
enough never to hide his eyes or wink
at what he was not meant to see: this room

is not his room. Suppose I tell the king
he is no king?
             "Arthur, I cannot sing. . . ."

Daisy

Daisy desired
the world on a string
Daisy demanded
everything
Mother and Dad
allowed her her wishes
hoping this plan
would prove judicious
but Daisy grew up
requiring a lover
soon as one left
she sought another
until she grew tired
of playing around
and flatly decided
a spouse must be found.

While most of her escorts
had thought her a dummy
several envied
her family's money
chief among these
was Warren MacFee,
whose style couldn't hide
duplicity
and though she was told
by Mother and Dad
that "Darling Warren"
was totally bad
she nevertheless
allowed him to court her
as even a proper
boyfriend ought to

and promise her castles
in the sky
that they would live in
by and by
until at each vow
her heart would sing

and she was eager
to take his ring.
Father stroked
his fierce moustaches
Mother lined
her face with ashes
they said they never
would abide it
if she loved him
she should hide it.

But Daisy simpered
looked demure
said that she
was surely sure
slammed the door
and went downtown
bought herself
a wedding gown
found a chaplain
avaricious
who gave no fig
for parents' wishes
then got married
anyway
on a gloomy
Saturday.

Sunday morning
Daisy gone
birds now singing
on the lawn

Father shaved
moustaches off
passed up church
to play some golf
went to work
on Monday morning
shining face
a woman's warning.

Mother washed
the ash away
took friends to lunch
and next a play
where she met
a man most charming
whose approach
was so disarming
that since they left
the matinee
no one has seen them
to this day
but Father brought
his typist home
and barely noticed
Mom was gone.

Later Daisy
came back teary
sobbed that Warren
was really dreary
though she had wanted
worlds on her string
she now was ready
to scrap his ring.

Father nonplussed
thought thought after thought
concluded next morning
he certainly ought

to do what he could
whatever it took
to improve Daisy's future
and set out to look
for a stock clerk called Mike
who worked in his store
a muscular youngster
who stood six foot four
considered by Father
extremely athletic
and likely to render
her case less pathetic.

Michael X. Murd
thought only a bit
and though like Daisy
not burdened with wit
deciding that he
should snap up the proffer
accepted Father's
unusual offer
to subsidize fully
a tiny apartment
where Daisy loved
the way her heart went
whenever Mike
caressed her bosom
swore that he'd never
leave her lose him
then bedded her lustfully
noon or night
even if
he came home tight.

And as for Warren —
well, what about him?
They're all doing
fine without him.

Decline of a Falstaff

" . . . at the turning o' the tide
for after I saw him fumble with the sheets
and play with flowers and smile upon his
fingers' ends, I knew there was but one way;
for his nose was as sharp as a pen, and a'
babbled of green fields. . . " <u>Henry V</u>

BECAUSE of sunlight shifting through a tree
the moving pattern silent on the shade
between my room and day
                                    invisibly
the sky escapes through holes that age has made
compelling in this summer heat that stirs
limp branches listlessly
                                    and I afraid
of light: the drawing of a curtain blurs
patterns: very soon
twilight beams will come
                                    interpreters
of something that was hidden in a June

The sound of nothing in the well
fireflies and heat-lightning in the hills
and a black tree in the night

STANDING by the bar
I became entranced by the scene inside the television
set, and found myself wondering if the tiny man in the
red uniform could really hit a baseball no larger than a
pinhead, and how far it might fly

A wideawake child
face hidden against the dark in the room
listening for
who's afraid of the big bad wolf
when he could no longer bear to listen
he opened the door

— So I said to him: Look here, it's all right,
there's nothing to be afraid of. After all,
there's only trees and heat-lightning outside:
it's summer, Jack. Then I closed his door,
hoping he'd go to sleep. But when I came
back from our room, down the hallway,
he'd started crying. Let me stay awake,
aunt, he called to me; let me go out
with both of you. I'm scared in here, scared.
I didn't answer, just went by as though
I couldn't hear him. What a goddamned nuisance!
I'm telling you, he is. Send him home,
send him home, let your sister handle him;
I can't, I won't try any more

Voices echoing up and up the empty stars

AND I have stood
on the decks of ferryboats at late dusk
watching stars
and counting time by the flickering
of neon in the brewery advertisements
sixteen to the minute
until the city was not sound
                        the not-city
five o'clock in the morning
sound
        of nothing in the well
        purple champagne
        castles in spain
        ain't it so funny we're lovin again

honey
you let me down
all over town
everyone knew you were foolin aroun
honey
gee I'm a sap
here in your lap
nectar in jugs and ambrosia on tap
honey
lovin you so
plenty of dough
back in your arms and we won't let it go

money:
        gray at their edges
nights twisted shabby fringes of sleeve
among the streets

mosquitoes beyond the elm

OTHER patrons
were uttering "C'mon, Duffy, park it!" when I realized that they had made a singular and possibly serious oversight. I scarcely heard their mumbling as I put my whiskey and water down again on the shiny black bar and dug carefully in my pocket for a cigaret

New streets new bars new jukes
the Stranger
        it is than anything green
        grass in dying parks
        his borrowed sedan at curbs
        the horses with sudden
        hard mouths, five ayem heard
        milk delivery
        whistle whistle bang clatter
        whistle

a leering lovesong to the gutter
urchin grown up now
to solicit trade from salvage — a red
dress — somehow illicit

THE SOUND of nothing in the well
beside the elm

old streets old bars old jukes
I Ain't Got No
Body, but just the same Jazz Me
Blues
          her eyes were
twinkle twinkle little bar
how I wonder where you are

what became of the big bad wolf
the big red wolf the big bad wolf

WHEN I had it out I made a great show of lighting it with my engraved gold lighter, hoping somehow to distract the attention of the grinning leprechaun who was hiding on the other side of the screen before his plot matured

in a thinning alley
          we can dream halfbaked
          tonight dreams can't we
who's your bigbuck honey
          honey
          pulsing with devotion for your money
          talks if no one
          else will to you, here-to-stay
          is ours and yours
          too, that is if you pay
          bigbucks
                    and go to hell

THAT summer morning
they found him in his bed,
a leaf between his toes,
the screen was still on the ground
underneath his window
when he left. They fixed it later.

An elm leaf

                      unparks
      his car and up the stairwell
      is the dawn
      curtains on the bay
      like a fog
              the green reflects
      from windows
      a taste of five o'clock shadow

And when he could no longer bear

the door opened

voices echoing up the stairs
who's afraid of the big red wolf
                          the stairwell
nothing in the well
          the sound of nothing

heat-lightning in the south

                      I had forgotten

Donald's Well

Homage to Edwin Arlington Robinson

I stopped to speak with Donald Marsh today,
and Donald, hoping for a bit of talk,
suggested that we both might drop around
to his apartment, "just across the way",
and share a drink or two. A minute's walk
sufficed to bring us there, and I soon found
that Donald hadn't lost his touch with gin
and bitters. When I asked him what was new,
what job he had by now, and all those things
politeness dictates, Donald's little grin
was still infectious.   "From your point of view
I guess I'm rather poor; tomorrow brings
great riches, though", he laughed; next, from a drawer
he took a gimlet and a little broom
and dustpan. Seeing questions in my eye,
he lifted up the rug, and in the planks
beneath were many holes. Then, with a sigh —
"I'll find it someday soon" — he drilled some more,
and, as I left him with a word of thanks,
explained, "You see, there's oil beneath my floor."

Dusk Storm

Leaves slide from the rage of air;
the mountains ebb to fluid shapes of black.
The day is little, and the lake
turns to running lead, and sinks far back

through eras to the flood. Blown dust
betrays old fingerings on untouched walls.
The torn, uncertain overcast
bleeds melting stars by ones and twos, and falls.

Emeralds

You wear these years of my life
like a rope of tiny shapes strung on my soul.
                  On your neck
pirouetting in your corner of mirrors
laughing tinkling catching changing lights
refract these fragments you have made of me
on the walls and ceilings of your private world.
                      Hell. Who can live
to live with the shattered images of himself?

I gave you, I remember, emeralds
which signified, if I had known it then
new unfaithfulnesses. Emeralds are only stones —
                      you wear them well.
Wear them well: wear them well:
I am the lives you twist around your neck
and take off sometimes when you break the string
and tumble scattered into your darkest drawer.

Emotion Does Not Derive from Any Form

(Student anti-Vietnam War demonstrations; composed circa 1969)

I hear you tell me to hate war:
dirty, people are likely to be killed.
I hear you all decrying in the streets
that men are forever killing each other,

saying there are other ways to take our raps,
devising your alternative love chants to be sung
at events created to be insistent theater
for parades of love.

Look, Spock's infants, resistors
in McLuhan's circuitry: there is no way for one
to love or to hate without hating and loving;
no matter what we are told

emotion does not derive from any form
of masturbation, we cannot turn on
love, nor even hate, each time we are assailed
by moments of incredible violation.

No use to chant of opposites in the street:
war and love are ravaging concerns
of the private heart: one may be damaged forever
by either, and one can hate them both.

Enthralled

They train her as their pet. They toss the ball
and say "Go fetch it", then lift up the hoop
and tell her to jump through it. And she does.
When she has finished with these tricks, they all
take turns caressing her. Next time, they call,
demand her presence instantly, because
they need to teach her where she fits their group:
submissive and obedient, locked in thrall.

Between, she sits up, human, begs for scraps
of love, but loving her is not their vision:
she has their leave to love them, but precision
is what they lust for. They want no relapse.
The most amusing trick remains ahead:
she must be taught to fall, lie prone, play dead.

Evocation

Let there be a tree
that, when you sit beneath it, will let go
one quiet leaf to mingle with your hair
and let there be a moon
that, when you speak to it, will sing for you

Let there be a star
that, when you look for it, will come to you
and rest upon your shoulder like a hawk
and let there be a wind
that, when you walk through it, will brush your skin
and pass so that you cannot be quite sure
that it has been at all or gone away

So let your nights be fierce with tenderness

Let there be a man
who when you come to him will come to you
so gently that your touching will be dawn

Fugue: October

Moonbeam-rippled field, autumn cloudfoam
at night's edge, and a rain
of leaves falling black as stars:
the negative promise. Through it all

September memories
and a counterpoint of April desire.
An organ sighs. Pity the frail musician
playing stoically none but the notes he sees

on the page before him: did we invent
a theme, develop harmony? Perhaps,
but counterpoint has become
a fugue tonight, and the lyric phrases

are bound by strictness, follow
the pattern: neverending, autumn leaves
as blackened meteors
falling low. Far off, the organ whisper

disturbs the stark trees:
they shiver. Tonight is cold, they say.
I answer yes, and holding you
still search for you somewhere near the moon.

Go Out in Anger

Your moon is edged with icicles tonight,
and they look sharp as daggers drawn from steel
that only flint can strike with sparks of light,
but flint is not too far from what you feel
if there is fact at all to what you say,
since I am not where you would like to be:
and what I am you think to speak away
and substitute an insubstantial me.

Go out in anger then to where you will
and do not talk of what you leave behind,
for what you leave behind may work you ill
if you should let it echo in your mind:
you might as well strike stars across the sky
as hope to order me to tell you why.

Heroism

The little boy, listening to everyone
gossiping near the store (because the drought
made farming useless), thought he heard the crowd
agree the aura of the sun foretold
continued heat. He'd heard his father hope
for rain next month at least; two zillion hours
was Uncle Abner's guess; but now the town
foresaw disaster in ten days, at most.

Recalling something he'd been told one day
by a mild vagrant who had spun a yarn
for bread and milk, the little boy became
a mighty hero: searching through the dirt
beneath a shaded rock, he proudly found
and killed a spider. Late that night, it rained.

Hitrun

Redlight, greenlight . . .
colorblind . . . explodes in my face
and I lie here counting raindrops
while an ant ambulance
races against the flood in the nightmare culvert.

Not a chance.

Holiday from Camelot

With hopes for dragons or for trout
he crosses streams like boulevards
and carries on his arm half pole half lance
to settle either form of doubt.

While chargers in the list still prance
awaiting combat and its rout
our hero takes a holiday from home,
favors no damsel with his glance,

does not respond to knaves who roam:
tomorrow is the jousting bout.
The chargers lodged between the bars bring pies
at least, or oriental foam

and lo! the tallest buildings dance
themselves to snowcaps near the skies
and schools are burning every class is out.
Now is forever and his chance

before the daemon world turns wise.
A very little kind of shout
proclaims the triumph of the good romance
the rain has ended and the skies

are blue beyond his wildest schemes
the rainbows filled with his surmise.
Floats hook and hopes for fire or flashing trout
in gutters flooded with his dreams.

In Another Country

In another country
the villages run southeast from the slow river
through fertile shallow valleys
where cottonwood grow old beneath cadenzas of birds.

No man there within the memory of men
has died violently by obscene accident or at the hands
of any other man. All deaths have been natural,
it is a place of Gods, the priests
have never yet preached ideals of retribution.
Crops in the valley have come up tall in most years,
a great number of the women are buxom
and many of their children grow to pleasing maturity.

Their only problem has been the meander.
At uncertain intervals of summers
the river floods with little warning; sometimes, too,
it runs all but dry in years when the rains
do not fall freely during the winter.
In seasons of flood or of drought
it is hard for the people to get quite enough to eat
and gnats, mosquitoes breed large
in muddy sinkholes
that the flood feeds among fields in the valleys
or that drought leaves in low places along the river bed.

It is a place of Gods nevertheless, where deaths
have all been natural events. But lately
more summers are lit by the dusty evening
lightnings of drought, and in other summers
the valleys fill up
with that rolling thunder which brings floods.

Some priests are withdrawing into the hills now:
near a few small springs between rocks
on top of the low red cliff, they are learning
to sharpen stones, with fantastic singing, and look
strangely down where men dare net fish from the river.

In State

After I died they dressed me and put me in a lined casket; they set me out in state for a little while so that people might see for themselves that death had at last replaced me as a reality.

Acquaintances came and stared down at me and I stared back at them, but to me they seemed shadows of indifferent strangers, and I was not moved to show them that I knew of their presence. Many people sent flowers, which were displayed about the room where I lay, and wilted just as surely as I had.

One old friend sent white lilies, which were placed at the edge of my casket; I watched the lilies dying in the heat of the room, and by and by I saw

a red ant

crawl down from one of them. I was suddenly mortally afraid of the ant: I wanted to reach out a wax hand and crush him, and exerted all the power of my will in an effort to do so, but he scurried deeper into the casket, and I lost him.

Later they came to close the lid, and someone said, "How white he looks in death, and how he stares!" But I was not staring at death, nor afraid of it, but of

the red ant

which had come out of the white flowers.

I Shall Think of You on Christmas Morning

With snow flickering tonight
among all the colors of light from the windows
of neighbors, I think repeatedly of the dark
wedge of geese last month in echelon
honking away southerly like two fingers
raised up out of a fist of clouds:
of other disappearances
and Christmases that never quite came true,
benedictions, greetings, seasons of emotion
that turn final as the hard wedges lumberjacks drive
to make tall trees split: all the forgetting.

And still I shall think of you on Christmas morning
among your world of gifts and the old traditions
that the shadows play with. And I shall will
you a sudden explosion of hard winter sunlight
to look out into from inside your window,
prismatic snow glittering among the trees
as the taut blue wind vibrates,
and I shall wish you various birds of winter —
titmouse, Christmas robin, a query of goldfinch —
all to leave you ringed in snow with a change of
                                                       symbols,
footsteps each one a delicate pattern of peace.

It Is Not for Nothing

I see you disappear in the snow
as if you had never been: and fear
you never were. Snow silent between us
swirls into a gray matrix
of parallel streets, footsteps no one hears,
night, time in the snow, marquees: lights
changed on a ladder by a shivering clown
who could not spell your name
                                        Now, Friday,
you have gone away bravely, disappeared, and the snow
melts on my face.   It is not for nothing
between us, and I wonder who you are, where,
drop bulbs that puff explosions in the snow,
climb down from my ladder, wash
clown from my face with snow, knowing
that I have known you
                                    No face is left
behind the paint for me, I am invisible
now I have forgotten the words, not even clown, I
remember only the shape of you
disappearing in snow
when I could have called your name

Jill's Answer

Jack and Jill
went up the hill
chasing a twinkling star:
they saw it sail
across the pail
of water that they carried.

Jack bailed it out:
it disappeared.
"I wonder where you are?"
Jack asked. The spell
broke loose: he fell
. . . from Jill came tumbling laughter

Jungle Gym

Tictactoe in three dimensions,
square on square. Recess ascensions:
youngsters finding new suspensions,
testing nerves.

Intersections: sideless boxes, corners
of air to be climbed,
laughed upon from the brinks of right angles.
An orderly universe.

Then, last night, our first snowfall:
new white waves fold the ice-blue shadows,
and gentle movements of air
stir crystal transparencies.

Best that our children play indoors
today: it could be chaotically dangerous
for them to know this sudden limpid spell
of curves.

Kobaleski

"With splendor caving in the castle walls
and Kobaleski's smirk concrete enough
to be a leer, at last I felt my time
to go had come. I thought I might retain
a few wild sparks within me for a crew:
at any rate, it seemed germane to risk
the sailing. There are seas: yes, there are seas,
but charts I thought I had would not be found
among the elements I'd put aside
as evidence of my inheritance.
I could not know what new expanse there was,
and I was here, and Kobaleski not —
as usual. Warmed by a sudden chill,
I tried to leave at once, with no goodbyes.
That was, of course, a social fault."
                                            He laughed
a brittle laugh, and Kobaleski smiled.

Krinkelt: 1945

In Memory of James Copeland

*But they have battled three times
through Krinkelt; and ours
was a farmland until November . . . .*

Now, manure and muck:
moon on February slush, snug homes
battered to wreckage by repeating warfare
through Krinkelt, and this evening
as the war moves on
I saw weary Belgian farmers returning home
to find their dry herds
tenderly mothering the lost, hurt tanks.

Life's Little Lessons

Life's little lessons
come and go,
brushing us by
like last autumn's snow,

all but unnoticed,
no rhyme nor reason
to visit so gently
so far out of season:

tiny flakes falling,
barely felt,
before they quietly
turn to melt,

renew the earth
beneath our flowers
still in their splendor:
late-blossoming hours

when daytime and nighttime
share equal division,
when we are not ready
quite yet to envision

portentous skies,
nor yet to assume
the onset of winter,
an end to bloom.

Life's little lessons?
It's hard to discern them:
often, indeed,
we never learn them.

Maybelle

The county clerk of records
tracing a rampant rumor through his books
checked and oddly
found nothing; meantime

her farming father,
together with her three irate
brothers, descended
on the railway station

of the county seat, but
the wary drummer, recipient
of a forbidden letter
some days earlier, cautiously

had traded routes,
and Maybelle kept her changing shape
close to her tears, while
several rural

farm boys and girls
having heard of her degradation
mocked her
and consorted bravely in the bushes.

The Mountains Over Mora

From the growth of a week of spring below the pass
in the mountains that stand impatient over Mora
I watched along the valley where Mora is
while the sun drained another afternoon away
and blue from the air
came down into the snow on the western mountains.

That day flowing away from out of Mora
left me whatever evenings bring,
suspicion of wizards and the tone of churchbells,
of wardens, the images of saints, and a coven of witches
that if there had been a saint then come to Mora
to try the labyrinth around my mind
would have cackled at the way the axis of the world
totters a bit at the pull of stars in winter
and the way green comes to the leaving of trees.
Evening called upon Mora as darkness gathers
around a stage at the exit of players,
and lights appeared to grow of another volition
among this evening. That was another year.

And now you move through my walls
like the ghost of April,
where I expected no one to come, to my sudden wonder
you roam where you will, and I must seek like the
                                        cripple
of a gone November through my own outer labyrinth
and can find no way through the maze to where
                                        you are.

I may never go back in the mountains over Mora
at springtime unless you should leave
                                        and come with me,
for seeing but me would frighten the hare from the hills
and the sting of any snake would cheer me:

and if then an assembly of witches in charge of
                              some saint
should descend on me with the design of rescuing me
they would find only the lost likeness of you
exploded away at the last
and the red heart and the crimson blood of me
welled up in a fountain to reach far out in the sky
enough to amaze that saint, and to test the patience
of witches, or the beliefs of wardens and wizards.

And the people then living in Mora
might marvel briefly at the setting moment of that day,
but among evening ringing of churchbells against
                              their mountains
not ever know what the lack of your presence means.

The Mulberry Bush

Jack lay by the mulberry bush
while cow contented calf;
through evening air and evening stars
the moon showed its lesser half

while the cow promised stars to her child
when there would be no sun,
and Jack made rhymes by the mulberry bush
till crickets forgot to hum,

till a dark cloud came under the stars
and rattled the mulberry bush,
till calf cuddled her mother close,
till through the anxious hush

the lightning bugs, the lightning bugs
whispered a different tune:
cowered Jack in the mulberry bush
while the cow snarled toward the moon.

Old Man

*For, and now in memory of,
My Father*

Look at you: a collector.
Now you keep records
of the records of records you kept.

Three quarters
of a hundred years, you
have amassed things: information,
memories, the memories of information,
the things that happened
and things that did not happen
but might have.
You try to recall all of them.

No less you have been a collector
of people. If it was easier then,
you think, people were easier come by.
Nowadays, you find a quality like stone
in faces approached and passed
on sidewalks, in faces
queued up impatiently together
waiting for tickets of admission.

Think of individuals
you might have met for the first time
clearing vines from their shoulders
in the overgrowth
of Yucatan among warm rain, in the Valley
of Mexico: stone recollections
of Maya, or of Toltec, infused
by an inexplicable aura of magnificence,
who were sometime believed to walk
as only gods may walk:

you might also know their faces:
they derived instead of gods from the farmer,
from the cousin of the stonecutter,
from the private soldier, perhaps
for political expedience from the king;
and encountering stone ironies in our streets
who are crossed by shadows of awe
at their own magnificence,
you may think quietly of dead faces
going to fragments in an interplay of weathers
and years, no matter the eventualities
that created them, humanity and stone
crumbling together,
decaying into the earth together:
stone recasts the face the mason saw
but the mason forgets.

When I was young
you exposed me to a rock profile
made by time and the seasons on a mountain,
another kind of face
you told me held the spirit of New England,
the men of that region. Now I wonder
whether I then engaged in the curious conjecture,
and useless, which way the spirit
flows, from the rock to the man

or otherwise. Or not.

Beyond you is my past. What joins us
you would say to me is these recalled events
that you put into your records
so I may remember them.

I don't see it.
It is the memories
no one has recorded, that you cannot keep
for failure to think of them again.

Filaments join you and me:
I am forty-five years
also of your past, and you never knew
most of what I remember.

Father, son, is a joke of temporal precision:
faces we have collected always
are some turning to stone; and some
in their various ways turn human.

Old Man: give over collecting
and all the recording. Father,
many things you may think of as going away
have never happened
and they never will happen.
We live like caught images in a web of concern,
each one of us tangled with other silent ones.

On Days When I Watch Ashes in Your Eyes

Dark as the dark between yourself and me:
on days when I watch ashes in your eyes
and feel cold come in you, then I grow cold
because I made the ashes where they are.

Wanting the spark to warm you with surprise
I look for other ways that fires may burn,
knowing fire may consume us totally
or only singe us with a gray concern

like smoke that stings the flames when they are old
and embers dull to broken flakes of char,
black as the black that masks your life from me
on days when I watch ashes in your eyes.

One Sort of Requiem

For "elle", with regret

You seem to echo borrowed attitudes
you think are new, but they are ones I heard
enunciated forty years ago —
maybe momentous then, now platitudes
that bring back gelid thoughts of snowball feuds
no longer worth the tossing, word by word
learned from your new-found friends, who likely know
them only from discursive interludes.

No aged quote from history can convince
all by itself: it needs matured perfections
thought through by scholars and philosophers
who weigh what happened then by what came since.
These friends whom you embrace are plunderers
of aging maxims, not of new directions.

On Hope's Eightieth Birthday

January 15, 2007

It is outrageously but undeniably true
as I sit here by a bookcase that represents
almost a fifth of my recently depleted library
that today is my first sister's eightieth birthday,
and that barely a few moments ago
I welcomed you, Hopie, to the society of octogenarians
over two thousand miles of instant connectivity
between where you are now and where I am.

Eighty years ago that would have been madness:
it would all have been shouting at village operators
and long-distance operators, lines forever disordered;
seashells in the left hand, black tulips in the right.
I would have done better to visit the local office
of Western Union and bespeak a telegram
for someone to hand-deliver to you in Florida
tomorrow or the next day — or whenever.

Easy now; so improbably difficult then.
You and I were born into times
of abrupt prototechnological technology,
not long after such futuristic concepts
as the application of simple electricity
to the megaphone: Victrola records, and sudden
bursts of words and even of vagrant music
interspersed with static in the wireless ether.

I remember, when I was a boy, exulting
to discover I had been born precisely on the day
of the twenty-first anniversary of the airplane,
of Orville and Wilbur's short-lived fluttering
over the sands of a North Carolina beachway;
and for years thereafter I was heavily occupied

reading stories of adventures in the sky
and carving model aircraft of my own design.

Aircraft, though, were transformed by science-fiction:
first in the "Funnies", the adventures of Buck Rogers
In The Twenty-First Century with Wilma and Huer,
fighting Killer Kane through interplanetary space.
Later, even more ebullient flights in pulp magazines:
Astounding Stories — indeed! — Amazing Stories,
Thrilling Wonder Stories, crammed with nebular marvels
created by fantasists dreaming for two cents a word.

Then the intervention of years: World War Two
nasty but necessary; nastier conflicts have followed.
Meanwhile children decided on their own what to learn;
teachers, schools, even universities, gave in.
Thus poor old Doctor Huer must have missed his
                                                education,
for when we reached the moon forty years ago
we lauded our achievement — but abandoned it,
only now to talk of going back.

And here we are on your birthday, reasonably deep
into the first decade of Buck and Huer's century.
No rocket ships. Happily, no interstellar warfare.
But life as it always has been? Not exactly:
this morning I pushed fewer than a handful of buttons
to speak with you in Florida; yesterday I talked
with Robin in Hawaii, and just last week
with friends in France and westernmost Australia.

So then, welcome to octogeniety!
Now is certainly not as we must have imagined it
growing up with our comic books, or when Nini
took us flying in her two-seat Waco biplane:
we have lived through unpredicted complexities,
but temporal solutions seldom lead to resolutions,
and even at eighty we are empowered to ponder
whenever we will, whatever happens: to speculate.

Only by Words

(in reaction to e-mailing)

Sometimes I cannot tell
whether you are putting me in my place
or being enthusiastic: it comes
from having two people like us
who were overtrained to be good with words
communicating with each other
only by words so many of these times:
only by words, without seeing
all there is to be seen as the words are spoken,
or hearing the sounds our words make
before the connections are broken.

Partir

It is so ridiculous:
   from where you are
the airplane pushed me away
into clouds,
the world stopped for a little
under them, lapse
of a few hours.

I come down
   out of the thin air,
measure in thousands
all the miles from you that I am now,
breath of our yesterday's conversations
not even moving
the brown bits of paper in the streets here.

So still.

Yesterday a wind curled
over us
from the plains
toward the southwest, there was snow
on the mountains though not its season,
when we joked we were solemn,
our lunch broken,
   it made no matter.

Here, metropolis: hospital,
cars clamor across the streets,
now the heavy grass
slowly dies, the airline
has lost my baggage,
my one-armed driver
buried
his cab in traffic from the horseraces.
Suitcase gone, missed

my appointment for supper, you
are still where you are, and I
am less than no where.
I tell you
I have totally spent my identity.

Do you know what I am afraid of?

:tomorrow

the one-armed cabman,
the luggage handler
who has sent my suitcase to God
know what destination, the pretty waitress
in a restaurant where any food
was as good as already entirely eaten:
tomorrow
they together will repeal all the laws
of aerodynamics, every ridiculous law
for mechanical motion

    so on the day after tomorrow
    I shall start to walk

oh, I shall walk my way
through adventures enough
    across the drying grass,
I shall be an old man
spewing spittle between my teeth,
verbose with thousands of miles of stories
by the time I reach you

    and you will not stay to listen.

On the Other Hand

*(a counter-poem,
composed immediately after* **Partir**)

on the
other hand
tomorrow morning
awaking
I may be
burnished
by vibrations in an early sun

a dream
you sleep with
where the moon is still

Paul Rejected

The mottled sunset clouds, that bring the dawn
of darkness, wrapped the hill, while all about
him fell the silence. Grayness flickered out
of windows as the valley folk put on
their sparks against the night, their shutters drawn
against the stars. Paul watched the evening drought,
and saw it drink the sun and leave the doubt
of darkened distances, where He had gone.

"Then tell us, learned Paul, how He could live
once having died." "If I could answer you
I would not need belief, but can one give
a rational account of facts which are
miraculous?" ("A worthless castoff Jew.")
The waiting stars were dim, and very far.

Playmates

When she was amused, he was amused as well.
She went her way and he went his at times,
but usually they found a way together,
happily doing what their whims combined
to lead them on to do: a joyful pair
whatever came, embracing each event
they planned or chanced on, even now and then
sharing a bed and all that happened there.

And then she left him, saying while she went
that it had been good fun, but she must find
more than a happy playmate for fair weather.
Now all at once he knew he loved her, fell
to writing verses, verses he tore up when
he reread them: verses that had no rhymes.

Poem 81

I have friends, contemporaries
excused from the constraints of time, of place.
Consumed by their own oblivions, they meander
among almost empty rooms and old hallways,
here and there a possibly comforting chair,
a bureau partly mended, a single picture
somewhat askew on a shuttered wall.
Very rarely all but silent echoes of merriment
evoke doubtful wisps of ghosts no longer familiar,
lost in all the shadows. No windows.

No windows. I know the early syndrome:
my head is overfilled with fragments, denouements
lacking preludes, events without beginning
and resolution. Details gone, and data
decades old, obsolete, while what I search for
is a current telephone number, even my friend's name.
Too much ancient junk there, sometimes, to recall
the real today that impales us each.
It is hard to remember what to forget
when we have forgotten all there was to remember.

Poem for John Meem

Santa Fe: December, 1969

      The dust devil
spirited you at Acoma one night
(in the year I was born)
                curious
in this country we have chosen to live in
that artists paint truth in the sand,
build monuments and missions out of mud,
invoke their ghosts by unremembered words

but Bach improvised with chords, Beethoven
searched fading echoes for what can be done with what
there is to do it with
                      and doing it:
John: you found ways among these changes

transience: transition: I am cursed with words
and metaphysics, but if I have a wish
I may wish for you, it must be: still
there are silent missions waiting that men dreamed
out from the earth for you to find

Poets Are Paltry People

Poets are paltry people, really:
forever dissatisfied, discontented, saying
life would be better somewhere across the street,
the railroad tracks, on the far side of town,
the mountains, at the edge of a different ocean,
around the world, at the other end of the universe.
                Why don't they go, then?

Poets prate unending nonsense about love,
but are usually puny perpetrators of it
if it should somehow sneak up on them:
they don't really want it, they want to moon about it.
What they truly need is a thick slice of beefsteak daily
if anyone would proffer it. But nobody
pays poets for their product, so they starve.
                Why don't they find a real job?

Poets these days can't even be bothered
to learn their trade. Their metrics are poor,
their rhymes, if present at all, presumptuous.
They ought to peruse our time-honored classics
to see how rhyme and meter should be partnered.
But they refuse to follow the best principles
from the past, from their proper predecessors.
                Why don't they study prosody?

Poetic ladies are just as bad as men. One will simper
and condescend, pose with a miniature magazine
no one has ever heard of, poorly produced
on inexpensive newsprint, in which is featured
a verse she wrote about bees on olive branches
in Genoa. Personally, though, she's never
been east of Poughkeepsie or thereabouts.
                Why won't she visit Genoa — and stay there?

Poets use odd words, too, in awkward juxtapositions,
one word has little to do with the next one:
combinations often aren't partnerships,
subjects and predicates often fail to match.
You can't figure out what poets might have been
                                                thinking of;
they pursue bad dreams, they presume on our
                                          language,
their sentences are often preposterous.
                  Why don't they learn grammar?

And poets are inept. They wear peculiar clothes
that rarely fit and are often unkempt. Smelly.
Invite one to your party: he'll posture sulkily
in a corner, talking to no one about anything except
his unique persona. But you'll note when he finally
                                                    departs
that he ate all the canapés he could reach
and also consumed more than his share of your
                                          chardonnay.
                  Why don't they have good manners?

Yes, poets are certainly liabilities
to our community. We truly don't need them here.
Poets are pathetic, male or female, failures,
unlovable, unlikable, no use to any of us.
They say we don't understand or appreciate them,
but as always they're mistaken. If one finally
does decide to move to the farther side of anywhere,
we'll be the first to fund a farewell fête, a festival . . .
                  The instant he's gone.

Recalling Astolat

Our lives keep taking unexpected turns;
scenes we expect to see again next spring
come oddly rendered, and the truths they bring
dissolve to truths more true than those one learns
in schools: to truths that void our days' concerns
by burning hot beyond imagining
in blazes that make ash of each fond thing
that we had valued, everything that burns —

but sometimes, too, to gracious truths, to joy
as unexpected as disaster was;
and after desolation cools, fresh land
emerges where new springtimes can deploy
their vistas and embrace us both, because
they bring perspectives we can understand.

Reunion

From emptiness of streets
he hails me, fondly greets
my wraith (he says): our loud
old laughs above mere crowd,
my match, his cigaret,
the quip we'll each forget.

Appointments: measured smiles
ambiguous through trials
and many errors, noise
mechanical, his boys
grown up since last we met,
his streetcar not here yet
but coming.
          And his grin
beginning to wear thin,
(at school his eyes grew cold)
the situation old
through recitation.
               "Dear
old pal, my trolley's here."

And all there was to say
reverberates away.

Rose Song

As fall was once an early sea of clover
and rain fell salt in season, so I lie
pale as an unremembered afterbirth
of carefree ages, stillborn on a sigh

that must have choked a tender heart to death:
it all is lies. His hands as mild as night,
your gentleman will steal what he can find:
no anger but soft rage leads her to flight;

and I am sacrificed to older furies,
for they who thought me meaningful were blind:
white rose too universal to be true,
too personal to be a state of mind.

Sailboats Into Eclipse

In memory of James Stephen Mikesh

Snowflakes across the sea, later
their white wakes lie absolute
across a blue world: evolute curves, plan
for a universe. Although

the afternoon expands, the cliffs
and sky expand, their slow sails
begin to burn, and gently
melt. Attaining dusk, the seaflakes

fade through the rim: beyond
its precipice, they trace last
tangent shadows across the sky,
and draw in the night.

The Seafarer

Translated from a poem in Old English

I may for my self   work a true song,
tell of journeys: how in troubled days
I often endured   endless hardships;
of bitter breast-cares   that I have abided;
of halls of sorrow   haunting the keel
in awful swells.   Often I spent
perilous nightwatches   at the prow of the craft
while it beat near cliffs;   bound by the frost
my outcast feet   were pressed by the cold
into chains of cold,   and cares chilled
my once-warm heart: sea-weary hunger
within my mind.   This no man knows
who lives on land   the fairest life:
how, wretched with care,   I weathered winter
on the ice-cold sea,   solitary victim
deprived of friends,   deprived of my kinsmen,
hung with rime-icicles   while hail flew in gusts,
hearing naught   but the sea-noises
and the sometime swan   on the ice-flecked waves.

The laughter of gannets   gave me pleasure,
the throat of the gull   out-throbbed the glee-man's,
the sea-mew's harmony   surpassed the mead-song:
when storms blasted   the stone cliffsides,
sea-swallows answered,   their feathers spray-splashed
as the crying eagles'.   No guardian kinsmen
but these remained   to mend my despair.
He who lives with delights   can little conceive
in his far-off towns   with his trifling misfortunes,
proud in his wine-dreams,   such weary years
as I in the sea-road   was sentenced to bide.

The night-shade darkling,   snow swirled from the north,
rime crusted the land,   hail crashed on the earth —
the coldest of grains — but my heart grew,
wise with knowledge   of waves' salt tumult
and lofty streams   I had traveled alone.
Now my mind's lust urges   on all occasions
that I in hope   adventure far hence
and seek the heart   of a strange nation.

Shadows for Shadows

Shopping in season, now I find
some wheels and coils and hands
and parts of springs all cased within
this cube of Plexiglas,

exploded but inviolate
steel landscapes brushed with rust —
a watch: it neither runs nor stops
and it cannot be touched,

frozen in its translucent age
as lasting as worn ice
at one pole or the other pole
where only random lights

intrude by stray refraction from
an oddly endless day,
and then are gone the endless night
while cooling stars mistake

shadows for shadows that grew old
before man thought of time:
counting our heartbeats to our graves,
each to his own decline.

Showering

I was standing in my shower this morning,
washing in fact my hair — what there is of it
has grown too long again, and I need
to have it trimmed — when suddenly
I realized that I was thinking a poem:
a poem of you.
                    You have been away
only a day, and in another day
you will be back, having — I trust — had
a good time in the back-country with your friends;
but already I miss our exchanges,
our more-than-daily e-mails, our phone calls,
our too-infrequent times together, exchanging
the events of our independent days, and especially
our very independent ideas.

You said it is good to have a pal:
so did I. And to be one. The only problem is
that when my Pal is physically somewhere else
and somehow entirely removed from communication —
a day, a week, hopefully not ever a month! —
the awayness opens a gulf in my life
that, no matter what I may be doing,
stays there: a hole in my person, somewhere,
wherever it is that my Pal resides.

I could give you a diary of the Friday things
that happened yesterday: up at four in the morning
to tinker one last once with my manuscript;
delivering it on time to the publisher;
listening to CDs of you reading;
an unexpectedly pleasant evening
at the party honoring the outgoing president
of our Foundation. But you were not there.

Simple as that: you were not there.
Or, rather, you were there, but only unreally,
just in my thinking. I missed you.

I miss you still this morning. Silly, isn't it?
But that, I suppose, is what palship is all about:
one cannot simply erase one's Pal
from mind, from body, nor from soul, I guess.
The lack of your presence at somewhere known,
somewhere we both have at least seen,
brings with it a sort of unhappiness
that I find hard to live with, especially when
there can be no kind of communication
to connect us in these absences.

You are not washed away with the soap and water
in my shower — must indeed be somewhere else,
somewhere inside me.
                                      Remarkable! I look forward
to being with you again on Monday afternoon. . .

Snow in Middle Autumn

Snow in middle autumn
coming today after Indian Summer
drifts in the air.

Silent louder than early thunder
on a humid afternoon
the snow swirls
between dark branches of darker trees
on which some leaves still dangle
                    and I wonder
                    why the quiet snow must fall
                    so soon.

Filling the day
flakes of snow drift to the earth
where they last
less than the time taken by a dream
before they melt

Some Things That Break

The past of me
having been all exercises in controlled passion,
experience has left no more to me than lines
in the sudden hand of a person no longer familiar
and tomorrows
gray and delicate as the last web
of a leaf torn by late autumn.

Too many years
spent: the cold comes on to destroy
leaves that lose the green memory of springtime:
the gift of myself to give may have been outused.
But my nights
are filled with imaginary conversations,
I would dream solemn nightmares of you

if I were a boy,
remembering you lost in my future;
my wasted dreaming could avoid nothing.
Even if tomorrows were mine to squander
I cannot speak
with this still you, I have conceived a curse of high winds
working in a sky more fragile than even the tendrils

of shaken leaves,
I cannot call on April to come and destroy us
with each other, there may be no climax
for experience lined by winter.
We are too intricate
with each other, growing together as the earth wears:
some things that break are irreplaceable.

"Song, Made in Lieu of Many Ornaments"

If I could turn each light that I can see
from where I am tonight into a rose
and leave them on your doorstep, you would be
bewildered by profusion, I suppose,
tomorrow morning when the sunrise grows
behind the mountains and you slowly wake
to fragrances you know you never chose
and many flowers more than you can take

into your arms. And if the world should break
in two beneath the weight of all I gave you,
it would not be entirely for your sake
that I would do what must be done to save you:
for what use is a half a world to me
if where you are should vanish utterly?

Suddenly:

This red river falling
through the badlands of my mind
will never reach
the dry lake of my heart.

Teddy's Crow

Teddy sat on a log and thought, and dreamed
as many spring-struck boys of twelve have done,
solving the solemn problems of his world.
Beside him on the log, beneath the trees
and moss and trailing vines and specks of sky,
Wilberforce, his educated crow,
derided all the tenants of the forest
in safety, from the cage that Teddy's father
had made for him. The crow's vocabulary,
though somewhat hard to grasp, was full of words
that Teddy loved to hear.
                                       But not today:
Teddy, on this afternoon of spring,
was thinking thoughts that seemed not to depend
on any words, but rather on trees and flowers
and birds and squirrels roaming in the branches
above his log. He had no mind to notice
the raucous mocking calls that Wilberforce
gave vent to every time he felt an urge,
for Teddy also had his song to sing,
a song he sang in little humming phrases,
soft bits of whistling, while his wordless thoughts
found echoes in the forest, cool and deep
and satisfying, till he was aroused
from reverie by Wilberforce's calls
taking a different tone. The crow, perhaps,
had seen an old acquaintance in the sky;
at any rate, he tried to utter something
that was not in the normal run of things
as Teddy knew them.
                             Teddy thought a while,
and found an answer for his friend's demands
at last. He opened up the cage and took

Wilberforce out from it, and wrung his neck
and left him in a grassy hollow place
behind the log.
                When Teddy ambled home
some hours later, just in time for supper,
his father saw the empty cage he swung
and asked him, "Where is Wilberforce?"

                                He shrugged,
and then he answered, "Oh, I set him free."

"Of all ungrateful sons, you take the prize!"
his father sighed. "Or maybe you've forgotten
the Saturday I spent to build that cage
to put him in, and help you split his tongue
and teach him how to talk, and you to listen.
Why did you do it?"
                      Teddy thought a little,
and saw the woods again, and felt the breeze
whisper the branches, heard the songs of birds
above the forest roof, and Wilberforce
trying a whole-tongued call with his split tongue
and somehow not succeeding well enough.

He put the cage away before he answered.
"I don't know. He seemed to want to go."

Tell Me No Lies of Roses in the Streets

For Harry M. Stokes, one of my students

Tell me no lies of roses in the streets
you took this morning, wary of your school
and fabulous escapes in airy carts
called up by disparate tutors: no such feats
for you these days, your life still ruled by rule
and by direction. Lessons have such parts
as differentiate them, make each one
unique; and, if you want to ridicule

the trolley that you rode, the flux of arts
you have not fathomed yet, or autumn sun
transmogrified by smoke, where are your answers?
The pavements know no rose but one that darts
from windowbox to its oblivion,
joining the pattern of the season's dancers.

Time Robs

Time robs the molting bird
of feathers that were warm
last winter, but which now,
in spring, he will not need.

And now you, too, have gone
Perhaps, some day, I'll lose
this lonesome wisp of me.

To Create the Gull

Suspended on intricacies beyond its mind
the gull is not sufficient, but depends
on lifts of air spun off by gusts that rip
smoke through the breaking bridges and wheel the rind

of scud from the wakes of freighters: cries amens
to tugs and ferries, fishers, while clouds build up
to brooding caverns set against the wind
where slow columns of darkness crease and blend.

And now is perhaps the moment I should trip
my camera at this taut solitude, this frenzy:
The gull there, the barren boats, the dark
clouds in the sky, across the bay the strip

of caught sunlight outlining the bent
wings of the white gull: and currents working
waves through the waste of water, weaving waves
through the broken clouds, smoke from stacks and vents

into a pattern with only the gull to mark
suspension, composed in white against the caves
of cobalt sky. But I think: not now, not yet
or maybe too late, the air is never still,

this water has hid a thousand derelict loves
and left them; again the smoke returns to fill
cracks in the sky, and if a sudden lark
should sing this sun on the gull would surely set.

To the Wind in Fragments

There is an impossible balance to every word:

I sometimes think when I speak
that the words I have said vibrate on cold currents
in the air between us, delicate globes
pierced by transient lights and skewed reflections
of the world around us.

In these fragile words that I say
meanings shimmer of things I have learned
from accidents, from the shapes of branches
in lightning, in drought, certainly in springtime
and from the colors in your eyes
and the downward slope of your cheeks,
from the gentleness with which some people
face tragedy or great happiness, from events
about which I know nothing real at all
except that for reasons I must never expect to share
they have happened, and from the ways
that persons meet, and often from the ways
we pass each other without meeting.

And some of what I have learned, I have learned
from the shape of streams falling southward from the
                                      mountains,
sending cold spray across stones and rock
in a rage of drops that disintegrate into mist
and rainbows among moss and among shadows.

I cannot talk with you. I have no tongue
but to utter spheres that shatter like fallen water
and release everything I have tried to say
to the wind in fragments that even I
do not understand when you repeat them to me
with a doubtful frown growing into your forehead.

I cannot talk with you for the brittleness of my words,
I am dumfounded
by this kaleidoscope of breaking globes,
by the interplay of fugitive lights
created by the most ordinary illumination
across their surfaces and in the hearts of them;
and among the fragility of them, I can hear only
tiny inner explosions while they shatter and drop.

Under many of the steps that I take, remnants
of what I once thought, once tried to tell you,
grind against the earth: I walk through shards
of visions I have had, flashes of understanding
that have become obstacles between us
by being spoken: I live such times
in a landscape of crushed, granular dreams
drab as last weekend's sleet
preserved by an unexpected coldness of the world.

Two Sorts of Trees

For Clarence Hodlmaier

Two ravens love to sit on the telephone pole
that goes to my neighbor's house. I watch them come
at seven while I'm making my daughters' breakfast.
They arrow around the pole, each taking his turn
to land on it while his brother makes do with the poplars
that the man who built my home
planted in order to hide my neighbor's pole.
I wonder if the ravens know
that one of my daughters only eats the bacon
and the other only the eggs? I eat both,
and sometimes at work I think of the ravens circling.

Last week, my neighbor told me he'd take the pole down
if I'd remove the poplars. I agreed:
the view from both our houses will be better.
Our piñon and our spruce don't grow so tall
they block us from the mountains, and now it's winter
the poplars and the pole can't hide each other.
At breakfast I shall watch the sunrise come,
and pay attention to what my daughters tell me.
But I shall miss the ravens when they go:
I think I ought to tell my neighbor so.

Waiting for Rain

One day she conceived
of painting a circle on the floor, and living
the remains of her life within it.

She debated the color: blue
like ocean dwindling
to the point of emergence
into the sky, the palest blue
where everything shimmers, blue
like the day on the shore,
tin pail bobbing on early waves
of a new tide, when the white birds
screamed cadenced spirals. Or red,
Ben's favorite color, telling her
it had a purgative complex
like the vicarious throbbing of immense
gouts of blood.   Or yellow for cowardice.

Then too there was a question of size:
how large the circle? What containments
might I still require, she wondered.
Speculatively she imagined confinements
available in her living room, thinking to choose
the corners to paint away, or all
of them, and whether or not
she might include the door.
The doorway rattled gently on the wind.

And there were also the cats. Should she
allow them to cross the boundary? Her white cats
created a definite problem: she foresaw
all sorts of difficulties training them.
But if she excluded them, who
would love them, feed them? Probably
they would come late afternoons, staring

at her across the quiet barrier
as if betrayed. Or maybe even worse
they might not return at all, having found
somebody caring. It was a dilemma
which was better: to see them grow
more translucent each day, become
entirely transparent, forget them: or to have
them forget her. Probably it will be wiser
to paint them in with me, she thought.

Mind involved from time to time,
it took most of all the morning
to design the logistics of her new event:
echoing door out, corner with Ben's photograph
tacked on a little slab of dry wood
in, in, with the folded bundle
of his letters, and the cats. Thursdays
she might allow time to shop, to bargain,
but no one else should cross the line, ever.

It was miraculous to have it all planned
at the end. She could hardly contain
herself to go for paint,
black, no color, the total lack of color.
But today, Monday, she never
went to the stores, and moreover
she felt rain coming: and so much better to wait.

Wartime Marriage at Shelby

For Adolph DellaCamera

When we arrived there, it was not so green
as other army camps we might have found
in luckier places. Everywhere the ground
had lost its grass to sand and dust, between
restive spare days when rain came: seldom clean,
a harbinger of mud. The pines around
our camp were not like other pines, the sound
of random winds in them seldom serene.

But you found someone near still binding you
to Hattiesburg, retraced familiar stars
southward away from your northeastern home
to her, happy to trade the things you knew
of brilliant lights and jazz for monochrome,
fiddles and banjos in illegal bars.

What I Remember from My War

What I remember from my war
is everywhere the coke aura of lukewarm fires
in London and Leipzig, in Reading, on cold nights
in Krinkelt and Kassel, in Paris, in Berlin,

and when I went away absent without leave
they never found me out, not in Germany
nor England nor in Mississippi. I made one poem
in three years, irrelevant to anything.

From Mississippi, I remember sugar cane
and watermelon, the swamp, Hattiesburg
and a small girl whom I named Joy,
making a second poem with only a word.

My best friend was shot to death in mistake
by his little pistol, an erroneous souvenir
he wanted to trade anyway, and there were verses
about that, once, a long time after.

Another friend died by drowning
near Schkopau at the end of the war: his boat
turned over before he learned to swim.
Loss has very little to do with poems,

and Joy, dear Joy: this is not a poem for you
because you probably never will hear it
and because you deserve more than any poem
but now is too late.

When the Winds Come

When I am very old I shall go away
and be a hermit in a cave in the hills
where no one will overhear
private questions I must put to the sparrows
hopping for the crumbs brushed off my jowls,
or watch the repeated events
I bore the chipmunks with, or see periods
of rime pass across my eyes.

I shall watch sunsets
with no comprehension of the colors in them, blind
at the sudden poignance of their going,
and I shall sit unfocused in the rain
with wonder at fallen stars
that leave the sky gray and empty
while they wash the dust quietly from my cheeks.

And when the winds come
I shall cry a little for the pain in them,
seeing the wild hawk batter his way
to the north, and leaves flying from the trees.

The Wife's Lament

From a poem in Old English

I utter this song   sorrowfully,
it is of my trials.   I must tell this tale:
how I've dwelt in grief   since I grew up;
older, younger,   and even now
my path of exile   is always dark.
My lord left his people   long ago
over desperate waves;   my dawns were moody
to learn what land   my beloved had found.
Then I turned to travel,   tried to discover
(homeless outcast)   help in my need.
But my man's kinsmen   made secret plans,
devised a way   to divide we two
widely for always   in the world-kingdom —
most loathsome of lives! — and now I'm alone.

My lord hailed me   to a home in this land:
few were faithful   on such foreign soil:
I had few dear ones.   And now I find
with soul-sickness   my lover sad
moody of mind,   mocked by fortune,
concealing his spirit   and set on revenge.

Full often we boasted with blithe promises,
that only death   would ever divide us —
nothing else.   Now that is changed. . .
nothing today   is as yesterday,
love nor friendship.   Be I far or near
from my dearly beloved,   his dislike endures.

They ordered me to dwell   under an oak
in a wooded grove   where a   cave was,
an old earth-hall.   I ache with longing:
the valleys are dim   and the downs lofty

the broken walls   overgrown with briars:
an empty home.   I am often angered
by my lord's neglect.   Lovers on earth
are living together: lie in their beds
while I walk alone   by the light of dawn
under my oak-tree   throughout this cave.

Here must I sit   the summer-long day,
here I may weep,   give way to hardships
that come with exile — nor may I ever
find rest in my mind,   escape this mood,
this weary longing   my life has found.

Man must always   have a sorrowing mind,
hard thoughts in his heart,   although he may hear
light-hearted promises   as well as longing,
sorrowful turmoil   if he trusts himself
for his worldly joys,   if he wanders far
from his native land.   If my beloved should sit
under such cliff-stones,   caked with such frost
deserted by friends,   drenched by water
in a dwelling of grief,   he would endure
mood-care enough,   and remember too often
a friendlier life!   Woe is the fate
of him who must long   await his beloved. . .

Wishing Well

Who knows where to find a wishing well
into which I might throw a penny, sure
of the outcome, sure
that my wish will come true?

Several well-intentioned friends will tell you
that I am too aged to be living on wishes:
am now at the time to be husbanding
such things as I have, not looking outward
toward whatever has so far remained unattainable,
so deeply unfathomable
that even a brand-new, recently-minted penny
will not purchase it. Resolution
comes at its own price, one beyond my treasury.

Or so it seems. Not a single new penny,
not even a fist-full of pennies thrown
into a neighborhood well along the wayside,
manages to turn itself by simple magic
into whatever it is I do not have.

Whatever? Whoever. No penny in this whole world
will grow a soul and turn into a princess
at any command I know how to make.
Not that I have ever wanted a real princess:
princesses these days are rare
and often turn out star-crossed.

No: not a princess. Simply another soul
to sit beside me by any old well we may find
and share the joy
of never needing to throw useless pennies into it.

Yesterdays: Tomorrows

Imaginary yesterdays
some new, some old, some spent
in doing what we thought we did
those places where we went,

are not in fact all steeped in fact:
we introduce a fiction
in all we think we know of them.
This might seem contradiction,

but we erase mistakes and failures,
recalling only what
we want to build our futures on
and not truths we forgot

because they seemed unpleasant or,
perhaps, inconsequentials;
remembering, when we search the past,
only our own essentials.

We live in visionary nows
where pasts and futures blend
into compelling dreams that all
uncertainties must end:

tomorrows promise resolutions,
but these defy foretelling;
they may be fables or may not,
and though they seem compelling

we cannot dare to plan on them
thinking they might become
more real than what is really real:
tomorrows are the sum

of all we want and wish and hope for,
the stuff of dreams we root
in fragmentary yesterdays.
There is no absolute:

our yesterdays and our tomorrows
are fables whose appeal
enchants us while we take account.
None of them is real.

Afterword

I hope that you were able to find something back there that resonated.

I have not constructed a great number of poems over the last sixty years or so, and the majority that I did construct have since been abandoned — many, indeed, obliterated. This is about all that's left: all the news that's fit to print, poem-wise.

I tend to work at poetry in phases, with many years in between. My five principal books and the majority of several hundreds of articles have been almost entirely about camera history and how to use cameras productively. Hardly poetic! Looking back, I can identify only three intensively active periods of making poems: the first during my college years and on into the early years of graduate school before I had to get into producing my dissertation; the second in the years that centered on the early 1970s; and the third beginning last year, in 2006. There have been a few short outbreaks in between, but they were exceptional.

And I've done a great deal of revision. Remaking. One of my earliest poems, the one that opens this collection, "Again and Always and the Stars", has been completely recomposed three times, even though its first incarnation did actually, if retroactively unfortunately, see print about 1950; and these various attempts at "Again and Always and the Stars" have even spun off an entirely other poem, "As If". If I don't have it right yet, it's not for lack of trying!

Something I've wanted to get off my chest for a long while: I grew up in school with teachers who persistently contrasted "poetry" and "prose". That's no real contrast; those pundits were too ill-acquainted with their subject to realize that the "opposite" of "prose" is not "poetry", but "verse". Prose and verse are simply two mechanisms for using standard words and grammar to approach your subject matter, two forms of the same language, so to speak. As I see poetry, it's in some way a slightly different "language". One can express poetry in verse, and most poets usually do so most of the time, but one can also express it in prose: you'll find occasional examples in the work of some of the finest novelists.

I don't believe you should try to create a statement as "poetry" if you can say it just as well (or even better) in prose. Teachers who assign their students to write a paragraph of prose telling just what a specific poem "is about" don't understand this fact. Nor do a great many of this world's versifiers.

Poetry is a means of fitting together words and grammar and anything else that is available in ways that enable the poet to use augmented language to transmit messages when standard language all by itself fails. Poetry is, in a way, a mode of deception: a mode that fools you into thinking in the way that the poet thinks, without explicitly telling you just how to do so. The person who hears or reads a poem is assumed by the ever-struggling poet to have some sort of receptive sensibility. On his own, it's quite likely that the audience member wouldn't have been able to verbalize what the poet has created, but once that statement exists the poet believes, hopes anyway, that his listener-reader will get the point. Thus trying to "summarize" a poem in prose is always going to miss the core of the poem. It's what isn't said explicitly that counts.

And when one sits down (or whatever posture one assumes for the task) to create a poem, the conception may come as verse, or it may emerge as prose. Either medium can serve the poet's purpose. For example, in this collection, the poem "In State" came to me right from the start as something that had to be expressed in prose: in its current "final" form it is very little changed from what I originally made it: it's in prose, but I think it's a poem.

More complex has been the construction of "Decline of a Falstaff". Again, from the start, my conception included some prose sections, like those of the activities (or whatever they are) in the barroom, but I also needed to have parts in verse. What I have wound up with is a poem (at least I think it's a poem) that incorporates blank verse, rhymed verse, free verse, and prose in order to achieve its effect. Prose is just as vital to it as are the other elements.

And, indeed, there's a lot more free verse in the poems throughout this book. My conception of creating free verse comes in part from my times as a very inconsistent jazz musician: when one improvises in jazz, one has to be aware of the underlying rhythmic and chordal structure of the piece of music on which he is elaborating in his improvisation. So it is too with free verse: creating free verse is very much akin to jazz improvisation. There is a felt rhythmic structure on top of which the poet pits counter-rhythms; there is a chordal structure of meaning and context and even word choice which controls the directions in which he "plays the notes" of his poem. If that basis of rhythms and chords and words isn't present as he works his way, his free verse will not be very compelling.

For an example: "Poem for John Meem". I was very fond of John, and greatly admired him both for his architectural style and for his work at preserving and renovating New Mexico's old Spanish Missions. I gave him this poem for Christmas, and he wrote me a long letter of appreciation. But he pointed out one adjective that didn't properly describe the noun with which I had associated it. The adjective was only one syllable, and there was another one-syllable adjective that would have meant what I should have intended; but when I tried the substitution something sounded wrong.

It was as if, on my saxophone, I had played a C-sharp when the harmonic structure called for a note in the F-diminished chord, a D-natural or a B-natural for instance. That whole section of the poem had gone out of tune, so to speak: I had to do something else. Eventually I recomposed three lines, rather than just a single word, simply to correct both the poem's fact and its sounds. Only then did it come out, as I felt, "right". (And neither adjective made it to the finalized version.)

All this leads to another suggestion. When you read a poem to yourself, try to hear it as well as see it. Pay attention to how it would sound if spoken aloud, as well as to what it says. Speak it aloud if you want. The sounds a poem makes are, or anyway should be, a very important part of the poem's means of communication. Sound, not just structure, is one of the elements that can often help us to distinguish poetry from prose.

Finally, a more personal word about sonnets, of which there are also quite a few here, with various rhyme schemes (and one in what is essentially blank verse). For whatever reason, I enjoy trying to make sonnets. The necessary word is "discipline". Sonnets force the poet to take a highly disciplined approach to his subject matter. Sometimes the sonnet structure is a help in organizing what one has to say; sometimes the necessity to find appropriate rhyming words, particularly in a Petrarchan sonnet with its two sets of four rhyming words apiece, frustrates one's intentions for a while. Occasionally a long while, like forever. A good sonnet is often very hard to construct; you should see all the ones I've discarded over the years! I hope that you've found one or two here that work between you and me.

You thought you were getting a volume of poems, and instead you've wound up with a long diatribe on one man's view of the "poetic art"!

* * *

Many friends and colleagues have given me help and encouragement during this long span; and occasionally some few have cooperated by telling me, of one or another effort, "That one stinks!" I thank you all. Especially I want to mention Professor Thomas P. Haviland from my undergraduate days, and also particularly Anne Howard, a fellow student way back then who has produced a number of children's books since; and Alice Briley, Jeanne Bonette, Marcia Muth, and Jody Ellis from the times when I was active in the New Mexico Poetry Society.

I have not kept very good records of when and where or even if many of these poems have been published. The majority, quite likely, have not been published at all until now. Regardless, I should thank the editors and publishers of the periodicals and books who accepted and printed what I had written. Here are ones of which I retain notes: *The New Mexico Magazine, The Sunstone Review, Encore, The American Pen, South and West, Encanto, The Pennsylvania News, The American Bard, Sandscript,* and *AD 1950*; as well as KNME-TV, on whose channel I once was invited to give a reading.

Peter Dechert
Santa Fe, 2007

www.ingramcontent.com/pod-product-compliance
Lightning Source LLC
Chambersburg PA
CBHW021016090426
42738CB00007B/803